EDEN OF VERSES

FLOW OF NECTAR

MISS. V. SIVADURGA

DEDICATION

The author dedicates this book heartily

To her parents,

To her family and friends,

To her non-blooded brother,

To the souls who disappear in Turkey tragedy.

Contents

Contents

Contents

Contents

Disclaimer

This cute compilation of 75 poems contain write-ups on various topics.

The author guarantees that the content is 100% plagiarism free.

Acknowledgements

"Eden of Verses" - a book of 75 poems came to the author's mind, when she saw many authors emerging out from the Creative Writers group. A sincere and hearty thanks to Mrs. D. Brinda, the admin of Creative Writers group. The author claims her hearty thanks to the members of Creative Writers group for mentoring and encouraging her.

She sincerely records her gratitude to her parents as they are the roots to all her success. She submits her heartfelt gratitude to her non-blooded brother Mr. KNR. Vignesh for his technical support. She delivers her thanks to Mr. M.Karthikeyan, Chairman, My Ladder Play School, Kuttalam, Mayiladuthurai dt., and Mr. N. Murugan, Executive Secretary(Retd.), NLC India Limited, Neyveli, for rendering a wonderful foreword for this book. Once again she thanks one and all who supported and encouraged her.

Preface

"Good friends and good books,

The wisest counselors."

Poetry is a form of literature that evokes a concentrated imaginative awareness of experience or a specific emotional response through language. Poet is a person who studies and creates poetry or a maker of verses.

As mentioned above, the author fills up her "Eden of Verses" with her imaginative awareness of experience and also with her specific emotional response. Many write-ups in this book are her own experiences and emotions. The author guarantees that the book will be a banquet for poetry lovers.

Foreword

N MURUGAN

Executive Secretary (Retd)

NLC India Limited, Neyveli.

I am very much happy to have the opportunity to view the book titled "Eden of Verses" written by Miss. V. Sivadurga and I am very much impressed by the quotes and poems in different titles interestingly.

I have gone through the poems and I really feel happy that the author has travelled in various segments of the life to experience in exile. It is really great to understand the human in the hearts of the authors depicted in her verses viz.

"Disappointment - Hurts a lot ,When no balloons was purchased, Stomach was starving,

Heart was burning, Eyes were searching, With the balloons flying, For a single purchase."

It is definitely showing the concern of the author about the down trodden people in the universe.

The collection of poems is unique in the sense that the poems are expressing the meaning in an understandable manner, what exactly it is meant for. All the poems shows that the author is very learned and has got immense versatile knowledge. The Author's mother Mrs. S. Sumathi, as Teacher, has got the Best Writer Awards, Woman of Excellence, etc.,etc., The Author, after finishing her degree, preparing for her competitive exams. In between this busy schedule, she has prepared this book.

I wish the endeavour a great success. And I Pray that a lot of crowns in the cap of the author in future. I wish her to bring many more books like this.

I wish her every success in her life.

N. Murugan

FOREWORD

Foreword

M. KARTHIKEYAN, M.ComChairman, My Ladder Play
School,Kuthalam, Mayiladuthurai Dt.

I am extremely happy to write a Foreword to 'EDEN OF VERSES', a book of veracity poems indited by Miss. V. SIVADURGA. It's my pleasure to be closely acquainted with her for over 16 years now.

Miss. V. SIVADURGA , I am proud to say, is a cherished daughter, very friendly, dedicated & committed, having qualities of high-flying and now happy to see her new face as a new age Poet.

This book contains heart touching poems and gives life to the words with divine fervor.

It covers and describes all the major emotions, help, respect, leaders, nations' symbol, relationship, culture, etc. Throughout the book, her magical words give mix-up feelings and able to envisage it.

This book should be read by anyone who loves Poems and additionally it will motivate the reader to become the new age poet.

Overall this book offers a variety of poems that are clearly written, well organized and enormously practical. It should be in everyone's home library.

M. Karthikeyan

1. Congratulations Let's Crown Ourselves

It's time to crown myself

For the achievements

From childhood till now.

A smart girl

Born to be known

All over the world

With my talents.

I crown myself for being

Patience and respect

To everyone who backstabs me,

For my love and caring
Towards everyone around me,
For helping and supportive
At all my worst situation,
For being responsible
For all the work and my achievements
For being confident.
If you fail in your goal
Crowning your own victory
It's a bliss feeling.
Crown yourself for every victory
To gain more achievements

2. Salute to all Gurus

Gurus are important in our life
They are the one who work for us
Without any hesitation.
Thanks to everyone
For guiding me through a right path
And letting me know everything.

3. Thank God, we are gifted

Thank God, we are gifted
With all the basic needs.
Thanks for everything
For my gifted parents,
For the shelter,
For the food I eat,
For the love and care,
For the confidence and patience.
We are all gifted
With all the basic needs.
Gift the basic needs
Who is in need of Shelter, food, love and care.
Gifting the alms to needy
Who is in difficulty
It's a great work to society.

4. A few words about CW Logo

An entry to talented people
Who doesn't know their talents.
Logo gives you more confidence
To write more and more,
To explore their write-ups
On a specific topic,
To write their point of view,
To share their feelings
On every topic.
CW Logo creates many poets
It is not a logo, it's an emotion to write-ups

5. That comforting hug

Hug – Powerful medicine
Not equal to thousand words
Feels the presence of love.
Father's tap, Mother's lap,
Sister's naughty talks,
Brother's ridiculous words,
Best friend's consolation,
Equals to infinite hugs,
Meeting and hugging the person you miss
The best therapy for a depressed mind,
Fixes the broken soul,
Brings smile in our face
Heals the wounds in the heart.

6. A walk in space

A walk to another universe

To admire the beauty of

The Majestic moon,

The Sparkling stars,

The Shiny Sun,

The Glorious galaxy,

With my favourite person

Two hearts connected with love.

7. Disappointed Balloon Man

Disappointment - Hurts a lot
When no balloons was purchased
Stomach was starving,
Heart was burning,
Eyes were searching,
With the balloons flying
For a single purchase.

8. Clouds

Clouds - endless love to the world
As our parents love towards us.
Soft and fluffy as marshmallow
But inedible to swallow.
Untouchable but beautiful to see
As different impressive pictures,
That attractes all age people.
When it is depressed
It is heavy and dark,
Falls as rain drops,
Hears our secrets as eaves drop on
Turn silent as nothing known
Watches everything from the top.

9. Head is a store house of knowledge not money

Knowledge-power of opportunity,

Be obligate to store,

Beautiful memories,

Not the gratitious circumstances.

Creative thoughts of the dream,

Not the thoughts of money,

More knowledge lots of lovely memories.

10. Flight experience

Flight - travel between clouds,

Whenever I saw a flight

I admire it as a flying kite.

From down it is small,

When I travelled in it

I admired that I had came to a new world.

I saw a cute miniature world

The love for the flight doesn't end at any age.

11. A day in hill top residential school

Top Hill School-a new-cool planet
Surrounded by ice
For the children who love school
With a new way of dressing,
Without a drop of sweating,
Wearing a sweater to avoid shivering,
With a two little plaits
And a cue beret,
Different people and
Different way of teaching,
Gains knowledge in the new cool planet.

12. School Break Time

School is a magical place
In that break time is a happy moment.
Break time = fun time
Playing in the ground
With our friends
Refreshment and canteen,
Roaming and chatting,
Snacks fighting and sharing,
Playing and completing homework,
Meeting other class friends,
Visiting staff in short time,
Lots of memories.

13. Lesson from my life

Don't expect the way
You treat a person
To treat you the same,
Be a person of helping mind,
Don't be a good hearted person
To safeguard yourself from hurts.
Life is full of temporary peoples,
So avoid believing everyone.

14. Giving alms to the poor and needy

Helping the needy people
Without any hesitation
Gives us lots of love.
They too needed love and care
Everyone of us need it sure.
People lending a helping hand are
The angels sent by God
To alleviate their sadness,
To reduce their distress.

15. Spread Love

Love, obligatory for everyone in the world
Spreading love is most beautiful.
From infants to elders.
Everybody needs love with more care
Spread love as a positive vibe
Wherever you go,
Whatever you do.
Make everyone remember you
The way by which you spread love.
Love is not injurious to life
It makes us healthy to live.

16. Life is Peaceful

Life is peaceful
When you lead it gracefully.
Life is peaceful
When it is truthful.
Body of two souls
Connected by hearts
Leads to peaceful life.
An half an hour happy laughter
With family members,
With friends and well wishers,
Helps to get relieved from stress
To lead a peaceful life.

17. Encourage All

Encourage - motivation

Encourage is a word to success

Encouragement gives us a great confident

Encouraging each and everything

Will lead all in a good manner.

If somebody discourages you

Start learning, run and succeed

That will be the great achievement ever.

18. King Maker Kamarajar

Kamarajar, the king maker,

A man of simplicity,

A true epitome of nobility,

A noble popular politician

Who fulfilled many people's ambition,

Showed the path of knowledge by free education,

Won everyone's heart by the work of devotion,

The leader of many revolutions.

19. Smile keeps you going

Smile - therapy to all problems
Key to the lock of everybody's heart.
Smiling in every situation
Saves you from many complications
To achieve victory in the world
Smile and keep on moving.
Somebody will be in pain
So smile with your 32 teeth everyday
To cheer up them.

20. Cock the best clock

Cock, the best clock

Punctuality is mandatory

To complete our routine work.

Do not procrastinate the tasks

Otherwise future will procrastinate us.

Thanks to the cock

For helping us in our success

By crowing daily.

Be a cock

Work without seeing a clock

To achieve high and get success.

21. It changed my life

The temporary world of fake people
Changed my life by insisting
Not to trust anyone.
An opportunity to reach my goal
With the help of my two souls.
Be a boss to your own life
Like a queen to your own empire.
Being fit and fine
Changed to a healthy life
By being patience, honesty and trustworthy
Everything changed in my life.

22. Greatness of father

Every father is different
To his daughter.
He is my first hero
With some common greatness
Which is done for his daughter.
He is my first love,
He is my first king.
Daughters first love
Whatever we fight
Safest hands to hold.
Best protection in the world,
Sacrifices anything.

The love towards me
Teaches evil and good
Doesn't change anymore.
My father is different in his greatness
Fighting like a Tom and Jerry
To irritate my mother.
He was the one who loves
His daughter unconditionally
With a sacred heart and love.
Helps me in escaping
From my mom's scolds,
Doing all naughty works together
To surprise my mother,
Expecting to be his friend
To share all my ups and downs,
Discourages me alot when I am down
To achieve in every field,
though he has lots of burdens and troubles
He doesn't say no for anything I ask.

23. My dear brother

My Guardian, My Protector,

My Best Friend, My Supporter,

My Companion, My Caretaker.

I don't have a brother

As a non-blooded relation.

I get jealous sometimes

By the relation of other brother and sister.

I wish to have a brother

To fight with him

Like a Tom and Jerry,

To protect and secure me

At my worst situation.
Happy to admit here
I have a brother
Not related by blood,
May god bless him
With all his needed chores,
And be with him at his worst situation
And keep him happy all the time.

24. To my dear Bestie

My dear bestie,
Our friendship is flawless.
Stress buster to my anger,
Pillow to my anxiety,
Hand to my loneliness,
Caretaker to my problems,
Crime partner in all my crimes.
We won't talk daily
But our bond remains the same strongly.
When we meet after a longtime
We create a happy vibe.

Hearing all my naughty talks
Without getting bored,
Helping in my critical time,
She can understand my feelings
Without asking a word.
I feel sad when you didn't talk
I am lucky to have you in my life
I am sorry if I had hurt you
Be mine always till my life ends
This is to my besties.

25. My Trio

My trio gang
My school besties
Spent together a short time
But created more memories.
We would not talk daily
But our bond remains constant.
There are more fight
But we won't give up each other.
Our two years of friendship
Mandatory till last breath.
Meeting up is difficult
But if we meet

Our vibe is totally different.
We will create memories
To be happy untill our next meet.
This trio gang
Became a big family.
I don't want to miss you both
Be with me in all my situation.

26. Golden days

Golden days = memorable memories

Memorable memories = rememberable moments

Rememberable moments = childhood days.

Childhood days are always special

No stress, depression, sadness, anxiety.

The stupendous smile of the kids.

The reason for the gaiety

Always loved by all.

Another golden days, school days.

Those were the days where

I laughed without any counterfeit

Friends, teachers, fight, love, exam, maths period,

Those ended in melancholy.

Now too I wish those days to come back

Where I was always active and free

Old is gold.

27. Paper Boat

Magic of paper
In the hands of grandparents
With unconditional love.
Making paper boats during monsoon,
Playing in the dirty rain water
By getting scolding
Gives a kind of happiness.
Float like a paper boat
Without sinking in the worldly thoughts

28. I overcome boredom by

I overcome boredom
By vibing to my favourite song
To chill up my temper.
I overcome boredom
By fussing with my mom
To be a person of calm.
Now newly I overcome boredom
By writing my thoughts
On a specific topic
To explore what runs on mind.

29. Mechanical Teacher

An updated version of teaching
Gives more attention in listening.
It's equal to the robot
Where there is no love, care and feelings.
There will be no past
As a teacher shares their past,
Can't express our feelings
As we share our feelings to a teacher

30. Love loses its value when

Love = Care+Respect+Honest+Trust

Love loses its value

When the two souls

Unable to achieve their dream.

When there is no mutual respect,

When ego enters,

When there is a untrustworthiness,

When there is a dubiety,

Broke the two souls into two pieces love.

31. Success and failure is a part of life's game

Life is a game

With more ups and downs.

Handle every situation with boldness,

Keep smiling always.

Avoid being afraid

Don't get frustrated

By the failure

Learn new skills

To achieve success.

32. I beat the stress by

I beat my stress
By praying to the god,
By listening to music,
By playing with kids,
By watching a farce.
Don't get frustrated by your failures
Don't overthink the ended affairs.
To be peaceful
Focus on your goal.

33. I remember

Memories are not good or bad

It's based on the situation

And how we take the situation.

Remembering the beautiful memories

A magical moment.

We laugh by remembering

The days we cried.

We cry by remembering

The days we laughed.

I remember the day

When my two beautiful souls

Join as one soul.

I remember the day

When my mother
Gave birth to a princess.
Some of my evergreen remembrances
The days of my childhood,
My school days,
My college days.
I remember everyday
Beautiful and lovely memories
Every moment is precious
Make it a memory
To blush when you remember.

34. When all my plans fail

When we enter into our life
Life has two faces
Birth and Death,
Start and Stop,
Happy and Sad,
Problems and Solutions.
When every step of my plan fails
I won't be in grief,
I won't get disappointed.
By correcting the mistakes of the last plan
I will create a new idea
With more conscious and knowledge.
Learn new things
To achieve the goal.
Make new plans
Whenever you get fail.

35. When I meet you I'll

Meeting a special person

After a long time

Is a magical feel.

After a long time

When I meet you,

My eyes will be with tears,

With a mouthful smile,

I will hug and kiss you

Without my knowledge.

When I meet you

I will expect to spend more time with you,

I will start blabber the happenings,

Sharing every happy and sad moment.
An outing at our home
By chitter- chatter continuously for the whole day
To create memories.
The days are incomplete without you
Can't express in words how much I miss you.
I remember the memories of us
When you are not with me.
That special person will always be
Close to my heart,
The love and care increases,
The bond exists till the last breath.

36. I am alone

Being alone is better than

Being with fake people.

Sometimes being alone will be difficult.

A good companion

Gives a good company

Even at our worst situation.

My best companion is

Music and my headphones

Making loneliness in to a vibe mode.

By being alone everytime,

We can achieve anything at anytime.

37. National flower Lotus

A mixed colour of pink and white
Which is beautiful and attractive.
Symbol of purity, strength and rebirth
Unique among ancient India
Propitious symbol of Indian Culture
A pride to our nation.

38. National animal Tiger

Magnificent creature in the world
Strong creature in the jungle.
Though afraid of tigers
Loved to see it in the forest.
Be polite and aim like a tiger
To achieve your goal.
Be bold enough like a tiger
To handle every situation
Be a beast in your life.

39. National bird Peacock

A beautiful bird,
With attractive feathers.
It open ups it's feathers
When it's the time to rain,
It dances by enjoying the rain,
Like a little child dancing.
Be a peacock
To enjoy every moment.
Don't be excited for everything,
Be excited for your positivity.

40. National fruit Mango

A seasonal fruit,

A healthy fruit,

Our National fruit.

Tastes sour and sweet.

Varieties of mangoes,

Helps in solving many problems

Liked by elders to youngers.

Don't be sour as a mango

Be as sweet as a mango fruit,

To solve every problem.

41. National tree banyan tree

A giant tree
With lots of branches,
A small root holds a big tree,
A big round space
To relax with peace.
Umbrella like leaves
Shadow that saves
From hot summer.
Be strong as a root
At any strong storm,
Be helpful everyday
Like the branches help in manyways.
Be strong as a tree in everything
To achieve the best.

42. If I get wings

If I get wings
I will help the needy
Like an angel.
If I get wings
I will travel around the world
Like a butterfly happily.
If I get wings
I will protect my family
Like a bird protects its chick.
Wings are like treasures
Lift and spread your wings
To show up how far you can go.
You may be with or without wings
May be with a broken wings
Never get frustrated
To achieve your dreams.

43. Never give up

Never give up your love,
Never give up your leadership,
Never give up your confidence,
Never give up your trust,
Never give up your patience,
Never give up your success,
Never give up on something you believe
While traveling through your dream.
There will be more failures
Don't quit when you fall
Run against the failures
To achieve your dream.

44. Life

Life is a book,
Book with pages,
Pages with lessons,
Lessons with thoughts,
Thoughts with optimism.
Life is fixed with two pages
First page is birth
Last page is death.
Between these two pages
We should fill
Our happy and sad moments,
Our success and failures,
Our love and kind.
Only one life
Past is a lesson,
Present is a gift,
Future is an opportunity.
Don't miss a single opportunity
A single opportunity changes our life.

45. Say cheese, for a click

Say cheese, for a click
Like a sun shines quick.
Say cheese for a click
For a sudden beautiful pic.
Save the moments as a memory
To blush like a baby.
While retrospect
Remembering the childhood days
Brings a smile suddenly
Without saying cheese.
Saying cheese for a click
With eyes full of tears
Bring the memories of school days.
Every moment of life
Has a cheerful memory.
Rememberance of every moment
Brings a smile
Followed by happy tears.
Say cheese is not a word
It's an emotion at all places
To solve any problems.

46. Mile stones for me

Starting from a small wishlist
Ends in achieving the big dream.
Milestone shows the distance
Between you and your dream.
Things to conquer
From a small corner
My uncountable wishlist
Going on an adventurous trip
To make my dream true
Wanted to be a virtuoso
At each and every field
Be a versed girl around world.

47. I think I like you because

I think I like you because
You have send me to this world - GOD.
I think I like you because
You give me free oxygen to breathe - TREE.
I think I like you because
You give me a fragrant smell - FLOWER.
I think I like you because
You guide me in the right way - FATHER.
I think I like you because
You care me when I am down - MOTHER
I think I like you because
You protect me at worst situation - BROTHER
I think I like you because
You're being with me
To solve all my problems - BEST FRIEND
I think I like you because
You are my best companion
When I am alone - TEDDY BEAR
Without these I am empty
I think I like you because
You all are the most essential
To sustain my life as confidential

48. I am busy with

I am busy with
Fighting with my dad,
Helping my mom,
Watching YouTube,
Listening music,
Dancing to vibe songs,
Making new dishes for my family,
Doing editing,
Writing my thoughts,
Chatting with friends,
Roaming with besties.

49. As a child, I hated

As a child, I hated
Being alone,
People lifting me constantly,
Pinching my cheeks,
Making me weep,
With their terrific face,
Doing extra curricular activities,
Doing homework.
As a child I hated
To eat healthy food,
To sleep when I was ill.

50. Disconnect from people who pull you back

Disconnect from people

Who pulls you back,

Who discourages you,

Who backstabs you,

Who gossips about your success,

Who demotivates you every time.

Disconnect from the negative people

Connect yourself with positive people

With more positive thoughts,

Heal the negativity

With your smart and silent success.

51. Things I learnt from my teacher

Things I learnt from my teacher
To be responsible like a father,
To be caring like a mother,
To be humourous like a brother,
To be smart like a sister,
To be a motivator like a bestie,
To be active like a kid,
To be intelligent like a topper,
To be creative like a backbencher,
To be bold enough
At every moment,
To be kind
With the needy people,
To be discipline
At all places,
To be confident,
To speak out your thoughts,
To be patience
Until your opportunity.

52. When I wear new dress

Gives unexpected happiness
With heart full of flying butterflies
Feeling like a princess
In the new dress.
Wearing new dress
Gives a new feel.
Roaming like a child
Around the world,
Creating memories
By wearing new dress
On the special day.

53. Gift

Showing concern
For the person you love.
Life is a gift from God
Being a guider is a gift from father.
Being a caretaker is a gift from mother.
Being a protector is a gift from brother.
Being a supporter is a gift from Bestfriend.
Gift is a treasure
Which comes from the heart.
Family is my first gift,
Bestfriend is my second gift,
My teddy bear is my third gift.
Best gifts come from the heart
Not from the store
Return every gift with a smile.

54. It's my fault, I'm sorry

It's my fault, I'm sorry
For trusting everyone blindly,
For loving everyone truly,
Who doesn't loves me back,
For hurting everyone
By the harsh words,
For being talkative.
Accepting the fault and moving on
Is a chance to new life.
Accept the mistake
You have done.
Keep on moving
Don't change yourself for anyone
Always be yourself and stay strong.

55. I'll take care of

I will take care of
My upcoming future,
My gifted parents,
My health and happiness,
My smile and beauty,
My stressed mind,
My all time loneliness,
My sleepless nights,
My obsessed thoughts.
Taking care of everything
Gives me great relief.

56. I could stay up all night when

I could stay up all night when
I slept in the afternoon,
The next day is my birthday,
It is my best friend's wedding.
I feel anxiety about my exam,
I feel depressed,
I get scold from my parents,
I overthink about my future,
I am going to meet old friends,
I plan to revisit my favourite place,
I have lots of work load.

57. Sundays are for

Waking up late,
Chilling out with music,
Without bathing and brushing
Spa at home,
Anytime eating food,
Plans to complete the pending tasks
But scroll the mobile full day,
Watching movies,
Disturbing my parents,
Unexpected hangout,
Unplanned shopping,
Scheduling the plan for next week,
Sundays are for taking rest
From the work stress of the past week.
A day to remember
The joy and sorrow of that week.

58. Nearby but faraway

Some relationships are faraway
But seems to be with us
In our thoughts
In our day to day life
Travels with us.
Distance friendship
Nearby but faraway
From the people beside us
Keeps us happy.
Our hopeful dream
Seems to be faraway
The daily opportunity is the key to our dream.
Overcoming obstacles and life's struggles
The new learnings to achieve the hopefull dream.
It is best to be faraway
You are faraway from me
Not from my heart
The distance between our favourites
Makes us eager to achieve it.
Good to be faraway sometime
But not everytime.

59. Laughing outside, crying outside

Yes it's me
Shifting from a happy, jolly, talkative person
To a dull human who is no longer interested in anything
Strong people laughs outside
But cries a lot inside.
I am the girl who cries the previous night
But smiles in the morning.
Crying inside in depression and hurting
To avoid my parents suffering.
Sometimes it is good to laugh
To hide our sadness.
People laughing outside is not happy
They are ready to face their problems
Being surrounded by sad people
It's better to be alone.

60. Bee and flower

Enter Caption

A beautiful relation

Connecting each and every moment of life.

Care and respect from the blossom

Enchant the bee to the gravity of nectar

A bee with starving tum

Hijacked some honey from bloom.

Words are like bees

Gives honey to ears

Bloom your dream like a flower

Success will come automatically.

Every moment of life is like honey

Enjoy and bloom around the world.

61. Fill up the box with sweets

Let's fill this box
With delicious desserts.
Cashew Kaaju katli,
Melting Palkova,
Buttery Mysur paak,
Hot Halwa,
Icy Rasagulla,
Crispy Rava Laddu,
Serving this desserts
To our loved ones
In an auspicious occasion
Strongs the relationship.

62. A stitch in time saves nine

Problems are part of life

Each and every day

Trouble comes in different way.

Solving the problem

At that time

Relieves you from stress,

Later the solution

Gives you mental tension.

Solve the problem

With patience and temperance,

Not with fear and anxiety.

Speaking without harsh words

To anyone on a problem

Solves every problem

Saves the relationship.

63. I wish I could escape from

From my dad's scolding,
From my mom to help her,
From writing assignments,
From my notebooks,
From my exams,
From my depression,
From my heartbreak,
From my loneliness,
From my nightmares,
From my uncontrollable tears,
From my worldly pressures,
From my past memories,
From my backstabbers,
From this society.
Escaping is not of fear
It's to relax from the pressures.

64. The last mistake made me realize

Making mistake is human nature
Every mistake must be realised.
Done so many mistakes
Realised it wholeheartedly.
My everytime mistake
Only being used
By everyone for their needs.
Trusting our loved ones
Trusted and disappointed.
After many grievences
Realised not to believe
Anyone than our parents.

65. Dear Pillow

Thanks for being soft and fluffy
To enjoy my sleep,
Sorry for all my devil dreams,
Thanks for taking care of me
When I am sick,
Sorry for the heavy usage,
Thanks for being with me when I cry,
Sorry for the depression,
Thanks for wiping my tears every day night,
Sorry for all the tears
Thanks for bearing all my sorrows,
Sorry for making you wet with my tears.
Thanks for being a second mother
At all my happy and sad moments.

66. Dear Post Box

Dear post box,
Thank you for your work
Through all over the world.
Thanks for connecting people
From different nations
By the cute letters.
Sending letters to our loved ones
On the special occasion
Gives a different feel.
Sending letters through post
A lot to share with our friends
In the absence of modern technology.
After the arrival of technology
Your work didn't stop around this world
Thanks for everything you share till now.

67. Golu

A day to remember
As navaratri in all houses,
To celebrate the victory
And to start a new journey.
A nine days festival
With decorative dolls
Narrating in a thematic way
Arranged beautifully in steps
Displaying to show the major deities.
Inviting youngsters and elders,
To make more festive
Singing devotional songs.
To bring a goddess
On this auspicious day
Festival of victory of good over bad.

68. I'm unique and special in

Talent is a gift from God

I'm talented in my unique way

By sleeping full day,

By eating everytime,

Getting scolded from my parents

For using mobile continuously,

For being lazy

To do all my works,

Irritating my mom

In the way of helping her,

Roaming here and there

Without doing anything.

My special talent

Drawing an art which I loves

Singing a song which I listen most,

Dancing to a song which I vibe a lot,

Editing a video for my photos

For the song which I love.

Everyone has a special talent in their unique style

Recognise and explore it

To the world with love.

69. Palmyrah Tree

The tallest and the strongest,

Leaves look like a hand with fingers,

Gives sweet palm fruit,

Stands strong and firm,

Even in a storm.

Be strong at any situation

Dream high as palm tree

To achieve high in your life.

70. A day to Thank you

Thanking everyone is a culture
It's time to thank God
For everything he gave us to live.
The treasure of kindness and love,
The weapons to protect,
The abundant knowledge and power,
The pen and pencil to write,
The food to eat,
The vehicles to travel,
The advancement of technology,
All electrical appliances and compter.
A perfect time to thank
Without all these we are nothing.

71. Let not one hand knows what other hand gives

Let not one hand knows
What other hand gives.
Every people shows
What they do to everyone.
Let not one hand knows
When the other hand helps the needy,
When the other hand gives gifts,
When the other hand shows love.
Make every moment in your memory
Not in your phone's memory.
Storing each and every happy moment
In your heart with love
Gives you a good feel.
When you remember it
Don't let me know what other hand does
Keep it safe with you.
Let everything be personal in this jealousy world.

72. Know what to let go and what to hold tight

Knowing each and every moment of life

Will not be good.

Playing each and every moment

With a miracle

Teaches you a lesson.

Let your past go

By living the present.

Hold your present tight

To connect a good future.

Let the person go

Who ignores your love,

Hold the person

Who cares and loves for you.

Let your mistakes be taught

Hold the upcoming opportunities

To open the door of your goal.

73. Online friendship is like

Friendship is a beautiful relationship
Online friendship is like an unknown stranger
With whom we couldn't shake hands
But connected by two souls.
Some online friendship, creates stronger bond,
Some are dangerous to talk.
Online friendship is by chatting and chatting
Gives you a feel of real friendship.
Online friendship are not good for youngsters.
To connect more people
Sometimes I believe online friendship
Sometimes I unbelieve online friendship.
Some online friends, uses some fake names
To mock their friends.
This creates a bad name for the friendship.
Make friends by looking at
The heart and the soul
Not by personality.
Distance friendship
Makes bond stronger,
Not for online friendship
Only for real friendship.

74. I didn't say anything because

I didn't say anything because
I was already hurt by the argument,
When my parents scold me
As it is for my good,
When I was disappointed
By my loved ones,
When my heart is at war with mind,
When my life is balancing well
Between happy and sad,
When life is too short to argue.

75. I express my thanks to

To the God who coined me to this world,

To my parents where there is the purest form of love,

To my brother who protects me,

To my Best friend who was always with me at every situation,

Thank you all for being the reason behind my smile.